THE FACTS ON HOMOSEXUALITY

John Ankerberg & John Weldon

HARVEST HOUSE PUBLISHERS
Eugene, Oregon 97402

Cover by Terry Dugan Design, Minneapolis, Minnesota

THE FACTS ON HOMOSEXUALITY

Copyright © 1994 by The Ankerberg Theological Research Institute
Published by Harvest House Publishers
Eugene, Oregon 97402

ISBN 1-56507-258-8

Printed in the United States of America.

01 02 03 / LP / 10 9 8 7 6 5

Contents

Preface

Introduction

Section I
Homosexuality
and Scientific Studies

Section II
The Bible and the
Homosexual Lifestyle

PREFACE

"I think anyone who is against anyone's lifestyle is just plain wrong." This common American belief has now almost become a national policy—one to be implemented at the social, moral and even economic level.

Why do so many millions of Americans hold the belief that it is supposedly *wrong* to criticize another's lifestyle? Perhaps because they aren't thinking clearly about the implications. Perhaps they don't understand how such an attitude, in working its way into national policy, has a potential to affect their own lives by harming society at large.

Certain lifestyles clearly do deserve critical evaluation because of their larger moral or social implications. What about the "lifestyle" of the repeat rapist or criminal offender? Or what about the lifestyle of the pedophile? The question, of course, is how far to take such a hands-off ideal.

Consider a recent report in *U.S. News and World Report*. It observed that pedophiles don't just hang around schools—they now "lurk around *inside* the schools." Among other things this article noted:

- Peter Melzer, a teacher at the elite New York Bronx High School of Science is on the NAMBLA (North American Man/Boy Love Association) steering committee and the editorial board of the NAMBLA *Bulletin*. The City Board of Education has known since 1984 that Melzer is a pedophile but has done nothing about it.

- Journals of sex research are increasingly upholding some of the basic arguments and principles of child molesters.

- Today "child molesters don't just hang around playgrounds, they apply for jobs at schools, camps, the Boy Scouts, Big Brothers, YMCAs. 'Boy lovers' love to work where the boys are." And further, our "culture is now so soft-minded that many will listen to any self-styled victim group, perhaps even pedophiles."[1]

5

6

So is it really a moral sin to question or be against anyone else's lifestyle?

As we documented in *The Myth of Safe Sex* (Moody, 1993), the individual and social consequences of the heterosexual and homosexual revolutions are appalling; indeed, the average American has virtually no concept of the overall cost, including financial, of liberal sexual attitudes.

Social and moral criticism of the homosexual lifestyle is no longer a conscientious option, if indeed it ever was. It is now a necessity, if for no other reason than the continuing spread of AIDS—a plague that, in America, is principally the responsibility of the homosexual community and, indirectly, their supporters.[2]

No one can deny a simple fact: Homosexual behavior threatens not only the lives of millions of homosexuals, but millions of other lives through the homosexual *lifestyle* that often includes sex with bisexual men and even heterosexual women, and also other serious problems (cf. Dr. Paul Cameron's, *The Gay Nineties,* 1994).

Heterosexual sins have also caused an incalculable amount of damage. But this is no reason to neglect the responsibilities of the homosexual community and its liberal supporters in America.[3, 4]

Introduction

1. How should we assess the sexual revolution?

In *Sexual Behavior and the Human Male* (1948) and *Sexual Behavior and the Human Female* (1953) Alfred Kinsey and his coauthors brought sex in general "out of the closet." These and subsequent studies taught many Americans a liberal attitude toward sex—in essence, that all kinds of sexual behavior (whether in marriage or out) were "natural" and to be desired. Apparently, the only "unnatural" thing about sex was the inexplicable guilt people couldn't seem to avoid. Supposedly, all that was needed was more and more talk of sex and more and more education for young people so they would not grow up with sexual "neuroses" like their parents. Sex "education" for adults (indirectly) and for school children (directly) became the vogue. In the end, tens of millions of Americans came to believe that sex among consenting adults was none of society's business.

Forty years into the sexual revolution, Americans are now beginning to experience the consequences of their being "enlightened" by a self-serving minority. Rampant adultery and divorce, increasing child molestation and organized pedophilia, widespread prostitution and pornography, militant homosexuality and feminist lesbianism, almost 60 sexually transmitted diseases, and some 50 million unwanted pregnancies leading to abortion are the result. By itself alone, the sexual revolution wrought the increasing disintegration of the family unit and with it the disintegration of society in general. Yet even now, the average American does not seem to recognize the *extent* to which modern society's major problems are primarily a result of widespread changes in sexual behavior.[5]

Now we face the swelling ranks of AIDS cases—in America alone over 275,000 dead. That is almost five times the casualty figure of the entire ten-year Vietnam war. About 400,000 more live with AIDS and at least 2 million more are apparently HIV infected. In 1994 alone, over 50,000 Americans died from HIV infection and that death toll will be exceeded in 1995.[6] In light of such figures, not a single person anywhere can afford the luxury of remaining indifferent to homosexuality or sexual permissiveness of any kind.

Unfortunately, there is more. A major Harvard study (1992) estimated that by the year 2000, just five years away, between 38 and 110 million adults and over 10 million children worldwide will become HIV infected.[7] Even this figure could be low. Dr. William Haseltine is chief of the Division of Human Virology at the Dana Farber Institute and Professor of the Department of Pathology and the Department of Cancer Biology at the Harvard School of Public Health. At his November 16, 1992 presentation to the French Academy of Sciences, this AIDS expert stated that without an effective vaccine or dramatic change in sexual behavior, "more than 1 billion people will be infected and will die of AIDS within the first decade of the next century."[8]

Innocent victims of the AIDS crisis are also increasing in number: preborn infants, spouses with infected partners, hemophiliacs, and surgical patients all face the possibility of HIV infection. The blood supply in many countries, *including* the United States, is anything but perfectly safe. In the 1980s transfusions had already destroyed up to half the hemophiliac population in France and America. Incredibly, even though blood officials in both countries knew or suspected the blood supply was deadly, they did nothing until forced into action.[9]

If no AIDS cure is discovered, if homosexuals and hetero-sexuals continue their lifestyles, if society does not institute appropriate restrictive measures so the virus will not spread throughout the general population, then the toll could eventually reach into the tens of millions in America alone.

Why weren't we warned? We were—repeatedly—from our own conscience, from our own experience, from the Bible, and from thousands of pulpits throughout the land. We simply chose to value sexual freedom above restraint.

Christians are the last to deny that most of society considers their view of morality irrelevant. But the fact remains: Had society followed biblical principles, there would be no sexual revolution, no AIDS plague, no millions of dead and dying.

2. How influential is the homosexual community in modern America?

Most Americans have little idea of the vast influence of the modern homosexual movement. Nor do Christians realize the number of homosexuals in their own ranks. In 1994, an article in *Time* magazine said the homosexual revolution "is still changing the way Americans see many of their most basic institutions—family, church, schools, the military, media and culture among them.... Everywhere one looks, there are signs of gay acceptability [formerly] unimaginable.... Gays are working openly in the White House and on Capitol Hill.... A gay man is president of the Minnesota state senate, and another is the democratic candidate for secretary of state in California. Pop stars and Olympic heroes acknowledge they are gay.... The gay dollar is courted by big companies and gay tourism is encouraged.... Earlier this month 20,000 gay men and women were made welcome at that icon of bourgeois family life, Disney World."[10]

Political Power

The homosexual lobby today has tremendous political and social power. Former congressman William Dannemeyer observes, "The effect of the homosexual movement on federal legislation has been stunning."[11] The homosexual community is currently pulling out all the stops to secure passage of local and national homosexual "civil rights" bills—which have already passed in some states.[12] In 1988 the Human Rights Campaign Fund, the homosexual political action committee (PAC), was the sixteenth largest independent PAC in the nation. In 1989 it became the ninth largest. Now it is even more influential. In light of the fact that there are over 4500 PAC's in the United States, this makes the homosexual lobby one of the most powerful political lobbies in the nation.[13]

Perhaps all this explains why some government reports now actively encourage homosexuality. For example, in 1989 the *Report of the Secretaries Task Force on Youth Suicide*, defended homosexuality as normal and encouraged numerous groups to actively promote homosexuality:

> A variety of gay male and lesbian adult lifestyles should be presented as positive and viable for youth. All youth should learn about prominent lesbians and gay males throughout history.
>
> It is important for schools to hire openly gay male and lesbian teachers to serve as role models and resource people for gay youth.[14]

In June 1994, *Time* magazine commented that "increasingly, especially for young Americans," homosexuality "is seen as a straightforward matter of self-expression and identity."[15]

The former U.S. Surgeon General, Joycelyn Elders, revealed her own agenda when she argued, "We need to speak out to tell people that sex is good, sex is wonderful.... It's a normal and healthy part of our being, whether it is homosexual or heterosexual."[16]

The former Surgeon General is wrong. Homosexuality is neither normal nor healthy. To have as an unofficial national attitude the promotion of unregulated sexuality in general is to participate in the destruction of our society.[17] Enrique Rueda points this out in his important and troubling text, *The Homosexual Network*. This text, we were told by insiders, has been effectively suppressed by the homosexual community:

> There is little question that the homosexual movement is part and parcel of American liberalism.... the preservation of traditional society and the values most Americans cherish does require the denial of the homosexual ideology. It is impossible to predict whether or not the homosexual movement will be successful.

Were it to succeed, however, the nation we have known would cease to exist.[18]

Religious Power

Liberals of all persuasions, including most liberal (and a few evangelical) churches, have also thrown the weight of their collective power behind "gay liberation" and "gay pride." Despite the fact that polls continue to reveal that 75 percent of U.S. church goers disapprove of homosexuality, liberal American churches have become one of the staunchest defenders of the homosexual lifestyle.

One consequence? Some have claimed that literally thousands of liberal and other Roman Catholic priests and mainline Protestant ministers are now HIV infected. According to AIDS expert Dr. Patrick Dixon, director of a national British network of volunteer help for AIDS patients:

> In the United States, government and church estimates show that up to one-third of all 57,000 Roman Catholic priests could be infected [with AIDS] and one high ranking Anglican has said that he expects a similar proportion of the United States Anglican clergy to be at risk also.[19]

Evangelical Power

Evangelicals Concerned (EC) is one major "evangelical" homosexual organization claiming to minister to evangelical Christians the "truth" that loving, committed homosexual relationships are biblical and in accordance with the will of God. EC claims it has thousands of members and boasts keynote conference speakers who have graduated from leading evangelical colleges including Wheaton, Dallas Theological Seminary, and Moody Bible Institute, as well as authors who have published texts by Zondervan, Word Books, and other evangelical publishing houses.[20]

Leaders of EC claim to have spoken at many conservative and mainline churches and to sponsor scores of Bible studies in major cities throughout America. A reading of recent years of the official newsletter, Record, indicates that the influence of this group among certain evangelicals is not small. Apparently, a significant number of evangelicals now support the idea that evangelical homosexuals have the moral right before God to live in allegedly committed homosexual relationships.[21]

Coercive Power

Homosexuals have learned that they can also wield tremendous coercive powers. For example, the 1973 landmark decision of the American Psychiatric Association to remove homosexuality from its list of mental disorders was, in large part, the product of militant intimidation by homosexuals—not to mention "spurious and pseudoscientific" reasoning.[22]

Homosexual activism has greatly influenced national public health policy. For example, because of gay objections, the testing, reporting, and tracing of AIDS are not standard procedures for managing what will probably become the worst scourge in history—even though such methods have been done with every other communicable epidemic.[23]

In addition, the national group called ACT-UP (AIDS Coalition To Unleash Power) has as a principal goal the attending of meetings and events where "the AIDS agenda is not to their choosing and either disrupt the discussion or else break it up entirely."[24]

The above listing comprises only the briefest spot survey illustrating the power of homosexual activism. Were we to discuss the fields of education, social institutions, psychology, cinema, art, literature, and others, the influence of this lobby would be understood for what it is.

As recently as 1961, *every* state in the nation outlawed homosexual activity. By 1980, 21 states had decriminalized sodomy; by 1994 27 states had done so.[25] In 1994 *Time* magazine correctly referred to "a quarter century of phenomenal change" in attitudes toward and progress of the homosexual agenda.[26]

In other words, what happened with abortion is now happening with homosexuality: Legalization implies morality. Everyone concedes that people will more easily engage in a legal activity than an illegal one. Yet the issue here is not as much the enforcement of the law as it is the message of the law:

> So why outlaw homosexuality if you're not going to enforce the laws rigorously? Because the law is one of the highest expressions of what we believe as a people. If we say something is against the law, then we are putting everything we have behind it—our legislatures, courts, policemen, all branches of government and all areas of society. Conversely, if something is not against the law then we say, if only tacitly, that we approve of it, or at least don't regard it as destructive to society.[27]

But no society will survive intact without an *active* enforcement of moral standards. This is now so obvious it cannot be denied. To abandon moral values so as not to offend those who are immoral is hardly the solution.

Nevertheless, what is significant about the above promotions of homosexuality is that they are largely based upon the idea that homosexuals are "born that way." Therefore, it is not even possible to reject homosexuality on moral grounds. Who can logically condemn people for merely acting out what they are biologically?

Section I

Homosexuality and Scientific Studies

3. Are homosexuals "born that way," and does it really matter?

Gay activists frequently claim they are born homosexual and that their sexual orientation is akin to something like eye color or lefthandedness. Troy Perry, the former Pentecostalist and founder of the Homosexual Metropolitan Community Church, states of his own homosexuality, "I was just born that way." In other words, due to biological factors, many homosexuals claim their sexual preference is inevitable and unchangeable and therefore the homosexual lifestyle is something society must accept as normal—indeed, it should be protected through civil rights legislation to prevent unfair discrimination against gays.

Consider how this idea of biological determinism has been increasingly utilized in recent years. In 1940 a mere 9 percent of homosexuals claimed they were "born that way." By 1983 the figure had risen to 22 percent. In 1990, it was over 35 percent.[28]

But this also means that even today, almost two-thirds of homosexuals apparently do *not* believe they are "born that way." If most *homosexuals* do not believe they are "born that way," why should most *heterosexuals* believe they are?

Regardless, if a homosexual really is born homosexual, the argument is made that society cannot reasonably expect him either to stop his behavior or convert to heterosexuality. It is unfair to expect any person to change what they are biologically. This means that homosexuality is *normal* and even *moral* behavior for a homosexual.

Consider the strength of the argument. If a person is homosexual because of an inbred biological condition, then he can reform his homosexuality only if he can find some way to alter his biological nature. But to date there is no evidence at all that such a profound physical alteration is possible. As a result, the homosexual is left without *any* hope for change.

The implications of this view are that because the homosexual cannot change, all aspects of society must change instead, including education, religion, and law. Biological determinism not only affects our general attitude toward homosexuality but also our approach to counseling and treatment as well—it is *useless* because change is impossible.

From this point, the argument logically progresses to legalizing homosexual acts. Not only must they be accepted as socially legal for homosexuals but they must actually be promoted as "normal lifestyle options" by education, since a certain percentage of children will *always* be "born that way."

Some have argued that the church itself must be legally coerced, if necessary, to abandon its "immoral" discrimination against homosexual behavior and adopt a position in harmony with scientific "fact."

But is it really true that gay men and women are biologically predestined to a certain sexuality?

4. Are the scientific studies claiming biological support credible?

Research attempting to show a biological or genetic cause-and-effect for homosexuality dates back almost a century. But over the years, no research has ever proven a physical basis for homosexuality. Clearly, some scientific researchers believe that homosexuality is constitutional. One often finds their reports happily supplied in homosexual literature. But occasionally, even homosexuals have reason to wonder about this conclusion. For example, in his *The Homosexualization of America*, homosexual activist Dennis Altman observes of a major Kinsey Institute study: "They are impressed with the considerable efforts of biologists, endocrinologists, and physiologists to prove this foundation; I am more impressed by the inability of many years of research to amount to no more than 'suggestions.'"[29]

We must also admit our skepticism over some or much of the current research. We wonder how many researchers are themselves influenced by the widespread but false idea that homosexuals *cannot* change their behavior and therefore may be inadvertently looking for a biological basis to "explain" their assumptions. In other words, is modern science being used in an objective search for truth or perhaps, rather, appropriated for "political correctness"?

If our reading experience is any indication, it would seem that most of the popular articles written concerning recent studies concluded that researchers had found *firm scientific evidence* that homosexuality was, at least to some degree, biological in nature. But this just wasn't true. Consider the most suggestive recent studies:

1) Dr. Simon LeVay's research at the Salk Institute

Dr. LeVay studied a certain group of neurons in the hypothalamus structure of the brain (called INAH3 or interstitial nuclei of the anterior hypothalamus). He examined 41 cadavers, 19 of which were allegedly homosexual men, 16 of which were assumed to be heterosexual men, and 6 of which were assumed to be heterosexual women.

Dr. LeVay found that some of the neurons in the hypothalamus region of the brain of heterosexual men were larger than those he found in homosexual men. He theorized that if homosexual men had smaller neurons, then possibly these smaller neurons were responsible for causing these men to be homosexual. Likewise, if heterosexual men had larger neurons, then possibly these larger neurons caused them to be heterosexual.

LeVay assumed that if the size difference in neurons could be shown to be true 100 percent of the time, this would be evidence that homosexuality was biologically based.

However, at least seven scientific reasons have been put forth by critics who reject his theory, reasons which most people have not heard.

First, Dr. LeVay's own chart, published in *Science* magazine, revealed there were flaws in his hypothesis. It even contradicts his theory. Dr. Ankerberg had the privilege of interviewing Dr. LeVay at the Salk Institute in La Jolla, California, so we have his recorded comments on tape concerning this. Ankerberg said, "Look, you have three of the nuclei of the homosexual men which are actually *larger* than those of the heterosexual men. If your theory is valid, this should not be. Second, you have three of the heterosexual men with *smaller* nuclei than those of the homosexual men." Ankerberg asked, "Is that true?" And he said, "Yes, that's true." So Dr. Ankerberg asked, "How could it be then, that the Associated Press reported that you 'had *always* found that the nuclei were larger in the heterosexual men and smaller in homosexual men?'"[30] Dr. LeVay admitted this was false. The popular press had distorted his findings.[31]

Second, no scientist has ever proven that the particular region of the hypothalamus under discussion causes sexual orientation. Consider the comments of Dr. Joseph Nicolosi, who specializes in working with male homosexuals. His book, *Reparative Therapy of Male Homosexuality*, has gained him worldwide respect as an authority in same-sex attractions.

Dr. Nicolosi emphasizes, "We're talking about a general area of the brain that has to do with emotions, including sexuality; but in this *particular* nuclei, we have no clear understanding of what function it serves at this point."[32]

So it would seem that first, whether the neurons are large or small is not a firm indicator, and second, no one really knows if they are even related to sexual orientation.

Dr. Charles Socarides, Professor of Psychiatry at the Albert Einstein College of Medicine in New York, also noted that "the question of a minute section of the brain—submicroscopic almost—as . . . deciding sexual object choice is really preposterous. . . . Certainly . . . a cluster of the brain cannot determine sexual object choice. We know that for *a fact*."[33]

Third, even if the anterior hypothalamus area of the brain could be shown to relate to sexual behavior, it still would not answer the question of cause and effect.

In other words, what if homosexual behavior *itself* causes minute organic alterations in the body, which are only *a posteriori* assumed to be a contributing cause to homosexuality? Scientific studies have indicated that behavior itself might *cause* the size of the neurons to fluctuate, rather than the *neurons* causing specific homosexual or heterosexual behavior.

Dr. Kenneth Klivington, assistant to the president of the Salk Institute where Dr. LeVay did his study, has pointed to "a body of evidence that shows the brain's neural networks reconfigure themselves in response to certain experiences."[34]

So the relationship between cause and effect—what affects what—is not clear. Therefore, the difference in homosexual brain structure—assuming further studies confirm LeVay's "finding"—may be a *result* of certain behavior and/or environmental conditions.

Fourth, the sexual orientation of the people that Dr. LeVay studied could not be verified. When Dr. Ankerberg and Dr. LeVay discussed the fact that three heterosexual men had smaller nuclei than the homosexual men, LeVay said, "Well, maybe some of those individuals were bisexual." Ankerberg responded, "But if it's 'maybe,' then you don't really know," and indeed, Dr. LeVay confessed he really didn't know. Some may even have been homosexuals "in the closet" who passed themselves off as heterosexuals. Because all the individuals studied were dead, we simply don't know.[35]

The fifth problem with Dr. LeVay's study involves the possibility of researcher bias. Dr. LeVay is openly gay and has publicly confessed this. He is also on record as stating that he set out to prove a genetic cause for homosexuality after his homosexual lover had died of AIDS. He was even quoted in an issue of *Newsweek* as asserting that if he did not find the genetic cause for homosexuality he sought, he would abandon science altogether.[36] *Newsweek* further quoted him as saying he is seeking to " . . . [promote] the idea that homosexuality is a matter of destiny, not choice" because "it's important to educate society" along the lines of biological influence. In fact, LeVay has now opened his own school for homosexuals and lesbians in Los Angeles to help get the message out.[37] In all fairness, isn't it at least possible that a scientist with such a personal agenda might subject himself to researcher bias?

Sixth, the interpretation of data and methodology used by LeVay are also questionable. Other scientists have pointed out that even the measurement Dr. LeVay used is suspect. Should the alleged influence of the nuclei be evaluated only by size—or instead, by volume, actual cell count, density, or some other (or all three) criteria? Further, what do scientists do with each of these criteria and what do they mean? The truth is that no one knows.

Finally, LeVay's study faces the problem of almost all research attempting to prove biological determinism: Lack of replication. This seems to be the Achilles' heel of all such endeavor, for it appears that, almost invariably, other scientists discover they are unable to replicate the findings of the initial study, which means that the initial study has proven nothing at all. No matter how widely the results are heralded as "scientific evidence," the "evidence" is either found to be elusive or, if replicated, subject to other interpretations which undercut a biological theory.

Concerning Dr. LeVay's work, there is no replication of his finding in any other scientific study. In fact, at least one study by Dr. Schwab in The Netherlands flatly contradicts it.[38]

2) Bailey and Pillard's study on identical twins

The second scientific study the media have used to propagate the idea that homosexuality is genetically determined is the finding of a prevalence of homosexuality among twin and adopted brothers by homosexual psychiatrist Richard Pillard and psychologist/gay rights activist Michael Bailey. These researchers recruited the subjects for their study through homosexual publications which cater exclusively to the homosexual population. Thus, their study did not represent a randomized, nonbiased selection.[39]

Nevertheless, they found that of the brothers who responded, 52 percent of identical twins, 22 percent of fraternal twins, 11 percent of adoptive brothers, and 9 percent of nontwin brothers were homosexual. Bailey and Pillard theorized that the reason there was such a high percentage of homosexuality among identical twins was because of their identical genetic makeup.

But here we also encounter problems. Half of the identical twins were not homosexual; they were clearly heterosexual. How could this be, if they shared the same genes that supposedly predetermine homosexuality? In *Perpetuating Homosexual Myths*, Richard A. Cohen noted, "If a homosexual orientation is genetic, then 100 percent of all identical twin brothers should have been homosexual, but only half were. Therefore, it is easy to conclude that environmental factors, not genes, cause homosexuality."[40]

Even Dr. Simon LeVay admitted that neither Bailey and Pillard's study on twins nor his own brain research has proven that homosexuality is genetically determined. "At the moment it's still a very big mystery. Not even my work nor any other work that's been done so far really totally clarifies the situation of what makes people gay or straight.... In fact, the twin studies, for example, suggest that it's not totally inborn because even identical twins are not always of the same sexual orientation."[41]

And again, we must consider the possibility of researcher bias. Like Dr. LeVay, Dr. Pillard is allegedly a homosexual. He admits that his agenda is to promote the notion that homosexuality is inborn and therefore a natural sexual behavior.[42]

The editorial conclusion of the prestigious *British Medical Journal* for August 7, 1993, appropriately summarizes the problems with all studies like those of Bailey and Pillard,

> Twin studies of male homosexuality abound.... Most of these results are uninterpretable because of small samples or unresolved questions about phenotypic classification, the selection of cases, and the diagnosis of twin zygosity.... *Definitive twin and adoption studies of male homosexuality have yet to be done.*[43]

3) The Research of Dr. Dean Hamer, et al, at the National Cancer Institute

Dr. Dean Hamer and his researchers at the National Cancer Institute claim to have found that "male sexual orientation is genetically influenced." Initially they discovered elevated rates of maternally, but not paternally related homosexuality in the families of 76 gays. This suggested potential maternal transmission of homosexuality through the X chromosome. Thus, the team examined 22 regions or "loci" covering the X chromosome of 40 pairs of homosexual brothers who had volunteered to be studied through advertisements in homosexual publications.

The researchers found that 33 of the 40 pairs of brothers shared identical genetic markers in five loci of the q28 region of the X chromosome. This led them to the conclusion that a gene or genes in this region influences the expression of homosexuality in at least 64 percent of the brothers tested.[44]

But the conclusions are just as suspect as in the earlier research. For example, a "substantial statistical nudging was required to get a 'fit.'"[45]

Further, scientific authorities in the area are not convinced any connection has been established. For example, Ruth Hubbard, who is Professor Emeritus of Biology at Harvest University and coauthor of *Exploding the Gene Myth*, comments:

> This study, like similar previous findings, is flawed. It is based on simplistic assumptions about sexuality and is hampered by the near impossibility of establishing links between genes and behavior.... Of the relatively small number of siblings in the survey, almost a quarter did not have [the appropriate]

markers. Also, the researchers did not do the obvious control experiment or checking for the presence of these markers among heterosexual brothers of the gay men they studied.[46]

In addition, an editorial in the prestigious *British Medical Journal* commented on the Hamer research as follows: "The linkage results are ambiguous.... In their original analysis Hamer et al placed the homosexuality gene eight centimorgrans distal to the most telomeric marker. The short physical distance between this marker and the telomere, however, renders this result questionable."[47]

The editorial concluded: "The claim of linkage of male homosexuality to chromosome Xq28 has wide social and political implications. Yet the scientific question is a complex one, and the interpretation of the results is hampered by methodological uncertainties. Further study is crucial to confirm or refute this finding."[48]

Finally, Dr. Paul Cameron and colleagues, after careful examination of this study and consultation with various experts, also rejected Hamer's conclusions. They pointed out:

> A correlation for specific genetic markers does not imply that a gene or genes *caused* the brothers' homosexuality. The results could be pointing to another trait shared by these subjects and disproportionately common in gays, such as promiscuity, exhibitionism, or other personality characteristics known to be associated with male homosexuality.[49]

5. So what about researcher bias?

Research bias is clearly an operative factor in many of these studies. For example: "Hamer disregarded information that countered his hypothesis—although he reported that the sisters of these brothers had a higher incidence of lesbianism, which fits the traditional psychiatric model of 'disturbed families producing more homosexuals,' Hamer ignored this finding to pursue his genetic interpretation."[50]

Consider also the following:

> Of even greater importance, the widely held belief that homosexuality is largely a matter of incest and

recruitment is totally ignored.... [Further] biological determinism cannot account for orientation switching. The two largest population studies in the field, done by the Kinsey Institute and the Family Research Institute, have independently demonstrated that most homosexuals have indulged in heterosexuality and a significant minority of heterosexuals in homosexuality.[51]

In light of the suggestion that at least one of the key individuals involved in the Hamer research was also gay, one questions what percent of researchers so interested in finding a biological basis for homosexuality are actually homosexuals themselves? If many are, it is not unreasonable to think that their personal lifestyle and beliefs may have influenced their research methods and conclusions?

Further, how many researchers in this field might deliberately hide their sexual preference in order to lend supposed scientific objectivity to their personal conclusions? Charles Silverstein, Ph.D., is the author of *Gays, Lesbians and Their Therapists* and has been a sex researcher for over 25 years. He maintains that attempts to cure homosexuals are useless because it is "biologically predetermined."[52] On the "Geraldo" TV show for June 11, 1991, he actually claimed the following:

> Geraldo, I've been a psychologist and sex researcher for a quarter of a century. In the last ten years, we have learned some things—and there's one statement that *every sex researcher* I know in the world will agree with and that is *sexual orientation is determined biologically.*[53]

Given this claim, one can only wonder how many sex researchers Dr. Silverstein has known. But this is not the point. For millions in the television audience, all they heard was an allegedly unbiased authority on human sexuality stating "facts" about how all sex researchers agree that homosexuality is biologically caused. Unfortunately, somehow Dr. Silverstein was never introduced with his full credentials as a *homosexual* therapist and researcher. Presumably, he never would have been had someone in the audience not asked the question, forcing a confession.[54]

6. Do many leading scientific researchers now conclude that homosexuality is not biologically or genetically based?

For over 30 years careful scientists have refused to assert that homosexuality is biologically based for one simple reason: lack of supporting evidence. In the following pages we will cite a wide variety of authorities to attempt to counter the prevailing sentiment on this issue circulating throughout society.

Dr. Joseph Nicolosi points out that he has examined the entire range of modern scientific literature relating to the alleged biological foundations of homosexuality: "I myself have reviewed all the literature, including LeVay's study, and I certainly don't believe, and I don't think any scientist really believes, that there is a biological predetermination for sexual orientation. There's much more evidence for early environmental factors that would set the stage for a person's sexual orientation."[55]

No less an authority than Alfred Kinsey himself, as cited by W.B. Pomeroy, his research associate, states "I have myself come to the conclusion that homosexuality is largely a matter of conditioning."[56] Perhaps this explains why sex authorities Masters and Johnson emphasize, "It is of vital importance that all professionals in the mental health field keep in mind that the homosexual man or woman is basically a man or woman by genetic determination and homosexually oriented by learned preference."[57]

Masters and Johnson also observed the following:

> The genetic theory of homosexuality has been generally discarded today ... no serious scientist suggests that a simple cause-effect relationship applies.[58]

Dr. John Money, leading sex researcher at Johns Hopkins University, reported: "No chromosomal differences have been found between homosexual subjects and heterosexual controls" and "On the basis of present knowledge, there is no basis on which to justify an hypothesis that homosexuals or bisexuals of any degree or type are chromosomally discrepant from heterosexuals."[59]

Even John DeCecco, Editor of the *Journal of Homosexuality*, says, "The idea that people are born into one type of sexual behavior is foolish."[60]

In the same issue of *Archives of General Psychiatry* that the Bailey/Pillard piece on the lesbian twins appeared, two highly credentialed researchers at New York State Psychiatric Institute concluded: "There is no evidence at present to substantiate a biologic theory of sexual orientation."[61] In fact, leading scientific journals have consistently pointed out "the lack of supporting evidence" for a biological basis for homosexuality[62]—which is hardly surprising since "genetically determined homosexuality would have become extinct long ago because of reduced reproduction."[63]

The fourth edition of the *Psychiatric Dictionary* observes that how a child is raised is far more important in determining sexuality than genetics: "Many pseudohermaphrodites and subjects with gonadal agenesis have been reared as females when their chromosomal sex is male (and vice versa); yet *in every case* the gender role and orientation was consistent with the assigned sex and rearing."[64]

Professor William P. Wilson—head of the division of Biological Psychiatry at Duke University Medical Center—argues: "It cannot be demonstrated that homosexual behavior is directly produced by the transmission of genetically determined behavior or by the occurrence of an excessive or deficient number of sex chromosomes."[65]

Dr. Clifford Allen concludes: "No investigations *in any sphere* indicate an organic basis for homosexuality, whether physical, chemical, cellular, microscopic or macroscopic."[66]

7. Is homosexuality really a learned preference?

If homosexuality has no biological basis, then it must be a learned behavior. Wainwright Churchill observes in *Homosexual Behavior Among Males:* "There are no sexual instincts in man. . . . Human sexuality is entirely dependent upon learning and conditioning. The individual's pattern of sexual behavior is *acquired* in the context of his unique experiences and [is] in no sense innate or inherited."[67]

Writing in *Sexual Preference,* Bell, Weinberg, and Hammersmith argue convincingly that "the experiences of homosexual arousal during childhood and adolescence and involvement in genital-type homosexual activities were very strong indicators of future, adult homosexuality."[68] This conclusion is underscored by the Family Research Institute of Washington, D.C., which conducted a national random survey of 4340 adults. In that survey, 96 percent of heterosexual males and 97 percent of heterosexual females indicated their first sexual experience was heterosexual. But 85 percent of homosexuals and 29 percent of lesbians reported their first experience as bisexual or homosexual.[69]

All this is why Dr. van den Aardweg, author of *Homosexuality and Hope*, noting the biological view "has become less justified than ever," concludes: "In my opinion, anyone who tries to approach the available physiological and psychological research literature open-mindedly will have to admit that the best fitting interpretation of homosexuality must be the idea of a neurotic variant [i.e., a psychological or emotional disturbance]."[70]

But further, an alleged biological basis for homosexuality isn't even the real issue:

> Are we to think that because something might be genetic in origin, it is therefore normal or "natural"? What, then, do we say about genetic deformities or birth defects? . . . Even if it can be proven that genetic or biological influences predispose people toward homosexuality, that will never prove homosexuality is in and of itself normal. It will only prove what we already know—that genetic variances can and do affect future behavior, sometimes in undesirable ways. . . .
>
> Let research conclude what it may about the causes; genetic origins do not justify sinful behavior.[71]

8. If homosexuality is a learned preference, does this prove that homosexuals can change their sexual orientation to heterosexuality?

Gay men and women are not born homosexual, and change is possible. Studies prove that homosexuals themselves *often* switch their own sexuality. In their 1970 report, the Kinsey Institute noted that 84 percent of gays shifted or changed their sexual orientation at least once. Further, 32 percent of the gays reported a third shift, and 13 percent of gays reported at least five changes.[72] In 1981 Bell, Weinberg, and Hammersmith also reported similar figures.[73]

If it can be shown that practicing "lifetime" homosexuals do, in fact, change their sexual orientation, this is a devastating blow to the claims of the homosexual movement. Here is what current research reveals about homosexuals changing to heterosexuals:

- Schwartz and Masters (of the 1984 Masters and Johnson Institute Report) revealed a 79.9 percent success rate of homosexuals changing their sexual orientation to heterosexuality. Their six-year followup rate was a highly impressive 71.6 percent.[74]

- Dr. van den Aardweg (1986) reported a 65 percent success rate.[75]

- Dr. Nicolosi told Dr. Ankerberg the following when Ankerberg interviewed him in 1992: "I have worked with about 175 men to date, and I can say in terms of claims of cure that when the men stay with me, in a matter of months they begin to experience change in their life."[76]

Even the liberal activist TV host Phil Donahue, a former believer in the biological theory, now tells homosexuals, "If you *want* to change, you *can* change."[77] Thus, it *cannot* be denied that homosexuals who *want* to, regularly *do* change their sexual orientation. Change can be more difficult for some than for others due to factors of motivation, will, and circumstance. But in actual therapy, with proper motivation and help, it would seem that change is possible, in theory, for all: "Abandoning homosexual habits, like quitting drinking, can be done and is done by tens of thousands each year."[78, 79]

According to the 1983 Family Research Institute survey of 4340 adults:

- 82 percent of those people currently lesbian and 66 percent of those currently gay said that they had been in love with someone of the opposite sex,

- 67 percent of lesbians and 54 percent of gays reported current sexual attractions to the opposite sex, and

- 85 percent of lesbians and 54 percent of gays, as adults, had sexual relations with someone of the opposite sex.

It would seem that not only are there more people who have tried and left homosexuality than those who remain homosexuals, but that homosexuality can hardly be considered unchangeable when the majority have been sexually attracted to and had relations with members of the opposite sex.[80]

Dr. Irving Bieber points out in the *Canadian Journal of Psychiatry*, "We have followed some [homosexual] patients for as long as 10 years who have remained exclusively heterosexual."[81]

Describing two books he has edited, *The Homosexualities: Fantasy, Reality and the Arts* (1990) and *The Homosexualities and the Therapeutic Process* (1991), Dr. Socarides observes, "These two books contain the work of over 30 psychoanalysts—eminent teachers and psychoanalysts and medical men throughout this country—and they all attest to the fact that homosexuality is a psychopathological condition that can be altered if someone knows how to alter it."[82]

If scores of different therapists and researchers over the years have seen thousands of homosexuals change to heterosexuality, and if this has been personally attested to by the homosexuals themselves and their spouses, on what basis can any individual claim that homosexuals can *never* change? And further, what are the implications if, as a society, we officially promote the nonchange concept?

9. Is 10 percent of the American population really homosexual?

Was Kinsey's research based on science or social agenda? The Kinsey Institute's widely reported statistic that 10 percent of the American population is homosexual is false and was based on faulty research. The most recent scientific studies have consistently shown that less than 1 up to 2 percent of the male population is exclusively homosexual. According to *USA Today* of April 15, 1993 (emphasis added):

> The notion that 10% of men are gay—born in the studies of Alfred Kinsey and popularized by activists—is dying under the weight of new studies.
>
> In the latest, only 2.3% of U.S. men ages 20 to 39 say they've had a same-sex experience in the past decade. *Only 1.1% say they have been exclusively gay.*

Drs. Paul and Kirk Cameron researched a new study, "The Prevalence of Homosexuality," in *Psychological Reports* (in press) that summarizes more than 30 surveys around the world with "large, plausibly unbiased samples" that reveal similar figures.

Kinsey never even *stated* that 10 percent of the population was homosexual. What he said was that 10 percent of men between 16 and 55 years of age mostly or exclusively engage in homosexual relationships for at least a three-year period. Only 4 percent of white males were exclusively homosexual throughout their lives.[83]

The Kinsey Institute currently is facing a lawsuit filed by Dr. Judith Reisman. Reisman accuses the Kinsey Institute of findings which, in part, are based on criminal experiments conducted by pedophiles who apparently sexually stimulated infants (as young as two months) and children against their will, without parental consent, for up to 24 hours at a time.[84] This is the kind of "research" that literally changed a nation.

Perhaps America should blush.

10. How may we best assess the homosexual perception of always having "felt" different?

The fact remains that many homosexuals claim that they have *always* had homosexual feelings and therefore never *chose* to become homosexuals. When talking with homosexuals, one hears this perception repeated so frequently it is easy to believe that homosexuality must be something inborn.

However, this self-perception of homosexuals says little or nothing about the true origin of homosexuality because the perception itself may be an inaccurate interpretation or foggy remembrance of something else entirely. The real question is, "How significant are such feelings?" What did those feelings signify when they first ocurred, and is it the same as what they signify now? Does the interpretation of such sensations accurately reflect a biological predeterminism or has it been colored or interpreted by homosexual experience itself? Further, such feelings seem to be readily explained by other factors.[85]

For example, Roger Montgomery, a former homosexual prostitute who appeared on "The John Ankerberg Show," was repeatedly raped as a young child by the homosexual man next door. Too confused and frightened from this man's threats to talk to anyone, Roger could only submit. But slowly, a transformation began to take place. What was initially a very painful and horrible experience began to be perceived as pleasurable. This was Roger's only experience with sex and what he apparently, for lack of a better word, "imprinted" on. This explains why Roger never had the perception of heterosexual desires. Through such experiences, his sexual orientation became "fixed," and he had little need or desire for heterosexual relations. This raises a serious issue. How many homosexuals can remember having only homosexual desires because this was the only sexuality to which they were ever subjected?

In other words, the homosexual's inability to recall choosing homosexuality may be only a half-truth. Human sexuality seems to be a neutral state upon which either homosexuality or heterosexuality can be written by experience or training. Roger, for example, was a victim who never entirely had the opportunity of choice. But even so, this did not guarantee his becoming a homosexual, as Roger himself later confessed: "It was a terrible mistake to remain silent, for if I had been able to share my situation with the right person, I am convinced I would have gone on to lead a normal, healthy heterosexual life."[86]

An inability to remember choice does not mean choice was never present. And even if it is not initially present, it is always eventually present. Homosexuals continue to make choices daily to remain homosexual. Whatever influences exist in a person's life—overt or subtle—which encourage lifestyle orientations, the key issue is how a person responds to them:

> [We] respond to these influences with subtle or obvious responsible acts of our own, adding our own choices to the host of influences that shape our personalities. We may fail to see the impact of our choices because the decisions that shape our lives are often not grand, climactic ones, but small, cumulative ones that result in our being kind or cruel, envious or thankful, idolatrous or godly.[87]

In conclusion, it may be that we will never know with absolute certainty a single or exact cause of homosexuality, but parental irresponsibility, molestation, and lack of religious upbringing seem to be key factors.[88]

> The complexities of the human personality and the influence of environment on human development make absolute statements about the source of the homosexual condition virtually impossible. Factors such as parenting, social and economic status, home environment, religious training, race, nationality, and temperament make the collection of data very difficult. The subjective nature of the topic also makes the interpretation of the data a very delicate task.[89]

The idea that homosexuals are "born that way" and can "never change" is a myth. It is a useful myth for many homosexuals and liberal activists, but a consequential myth for the rest of us. No one can deny that the claims for biological determinism and a 10 percent incidence of homosexuality have a great deal of political significance because they have been used to "justify" an entire civil rights movement. Unfortunately, these myths are fueled by a social agenda that has not been in the best interests of our nation.

Section II

The Bible and the Homosexual Lifestyle

11. Is the Christian church increasingly accepting the homosexual lifestyle?

In *The Homosexual Network,* Enrique Rueda reveals:

> Strenuous efforts are made by "liberated" homosexuals within the various religious bodies...to alter the teachings and practices of these organizations for the benefit of the movement....mainline Protestant denominations are notorious for their willingness to compromise with the homosexual movement.... Most denominations have "gay caucuses" or similar organizations which advocate the homosexual cause within the denomination.[90]

Mel White is one example of the influence of homosexuality in the church. White was a committed homosexual at the same time he was writing best-selling Christian books and producing award-winning evangelistic films. As recalled in his autobiography, *Stranger at the Gate*, his services as a ghost writer involved books for Jerry Falwell, Pat Robertson, W.A. Criswell, and Billy Graham. He also produced films with the late Dr. Francis Schaeffer and D. James Kennedy.

It was not until June of 1993 when White was appointed dean of the largest gay and lesbian church in the world, Cathedral of Hope in Dallas, Texas, that his commitment to homosexuality attracted national attention and most evangelicals learned of his sexual preference.

Unfortunately, White's rejection of biblical passages and attack upon evangelicals who teach that homosexuality is a sin have caused confusion and turmoil in the lives of some Christians who are struggling with their own sexual identity. Personal agendas of this type, which attempt to justify the homosexual lifestyle for Christians and non-Christians alike, have only led to thousands of people dying of AIDS. Regardless, the influence of such "evangelicals" like White or Ralph Blair, founder of "Evangelicals Concerned," are proof that the church must effectively deal with this whole area—not only with compassion for those trapped in homosexuality, but with full commitment to biblical teaching.

In recent years the Christian homosexual community has challenged the orthodox teaching of the church. In Europe this has been spearheaded by what has been known as the Gay Christian Movement; in America, by Evangelicals Concerned, the Metropolitan Community Churches, and related homosexual groups.

In a November 1989 debate on "The John Ankerberg Show," Episcopal Bishop John Spong argued that "homosexuality [is] being debated in every major body of Christendom—in every one of them—a hundred years ago it was not debated. It was not debated because it was the general consensus that it was self-evidently evil...it is being debated even in the Southern Baptist Church. It's being debated today because we are not quite so certain. When you're not certain, brothers and sisters, don't condemn."[91] But wait a minute. What are the underlying reasons for such a debate? Is it because genuine Christians are really having second thoughts, or rather is it because liberal elements within virtually all denominations are confused morally and have accepted the spurious arguments of the secular sciences and the "Christian" gay community? We think an objective evaluation of the situation leaves no room for doubt.

Granted, even some evangelical Christians are confused on this issue, but this confusion is itself a result of their being misled by false arguments or their own sexual confusion.

Among those false arguments are the following, to which we have appended brief responses: 1) that homosexuality is too common for society to condemn it (what about rape, adultery and other common practices that are morally wrong?); 2) the homosexual has the right to do with his body as he or she pleases (what about AIDS?); 3) homosexuality is a civil right (a moral wrong can never be a civil right);

4) critics of homosexuality are bigots or latent homosexuals suppressing their own fears (how convenient!); 5) homosexuality is normal for homosexuals; therefore it is right for homosexuals (the same can be argued for habitual criminals); 6) when society condemns homosexuality, it only damages itself because homosexuals constitute productive members of society (to the contrary[92]); 7) the Christian view of homosexuality is outdated by modern research (to the contrary[93]); 8) love is the only real issue (who defines love and its limits? Can sinful behavior be loving?); 9) Jesus Himself never condemned homosexuality (not so—Jesus upheld the divine authority of the Old Testament in John 17:17; also cf. Matthew 19:4,5); 10) homosexual behavior among animals proves homosexuality is a natural biological/evolutionary condition (not so[94]—regardless, men and women aren't animals); and 11) Christians, at least, must distinguish between the promiscuous homosexual act (sinful) and the homosexual condition (not sinful)—therefore monogamous homosexuality is not sinful (not so[95]; see below).

Once confused Christians are given the facts, they return to a biblical position. The few self-proclaimed evangelicals who remain confused on the issue do so not because of biblical teaching, but in spite of it. Their reasons for accepting homosexuality have nothing to do with Scripture but only their own preferences.

Regardless, the mainline churches themselves bear a significant measure of responsibility for the current condition of homosexual acceptance, *including* the spread of AIDS. To the degree that church denominations, congresses, and/or studies have *falsely* interpreted the Scriptures and actively *encouraged* homosexuality, they have simultaneously encouraged both sin and God's judgment upon sin. It is a sad commentary indeed when the very church whose mission is to support life and godliness is at the forefront of promoting sin and death.

12. What is the basic premise underlying the homosexual interpretation of Scripture?

For homosexuals, the fundamental argument is that when the Bible is understood "properly," it does not condemn homosexuality in itself. At most, it condemns only homosexual promiscuity—typically related to ancient cultic prostitution. The argument is therefore *historical*. Because the biblical passages on homosexuality dealt with specific

historical situations in the ancient *past*, they are "culturally conditioned" and no longer relevant for Christian
sexual ethics of the *present*.

What this means is that every biblical reference allegedly
condemning homosexuality as sin has been wrongly interpreted by the Church. For almost 3500 years the Jews (and
for 2000 years the Christians) have falsely interpreted their
own Scriptures, even though, on their surface, these Scriptures are plain in their teachings. Modern homosexuals
couldn't be more satisfied if they had written the entire
Bible themselves.

13. What are the basic problems of the "cultural condi-
tioning" argument?

First, the scriptural rejection of homosexuality is based
primarily on the Genesis creation account, which applies to
all cultures. This account *predates* the Mosaic law and
Israel's theocracy, and therefore is *not* culturally bound.

The scriptural rejection of homosexuality is based squarely
on God's original creation of man as male and female, and on
His instituting of heterosexual marriage and the family—
something upheld by Jesus (Matthew 19:4,5). Because it is a
teaching that transcends culture, it cannot be relegated as
obsolete by culture.

Second, what Scripture teaches morally in the Old Testament, it also teaches morally in the New Testament. This
uniformity also proves that these Scriptures transcend
alleged cultural limitations. Because God's holy character
never changes, His moral law never changes. God is sover-
eign over culture, not subject to it. Society's changing
values do not change God's moral law, which is valid for any
and every culture regardless of its beliefs.

Indeed, when God wishes to specify that something is
temporal or "culturally conditioned," He does so. For
example, the ceremonial aspects of the law of Moses that
were instituted in the Old Testament are rescinded in the
New Testament. From this we may conclude that if God's
prohibitions against homosexuality were restricted to specific times or practices and no longer relevant, God would
certainly have told us so in the New Testament.

Finally, the culture argument backfires. All cultures
have placed limits on homosexuality, and *no* known culture
has ever permitted preferential homosexuality for most
adults for the major portion of the life cycle.[96]

Some of the most liberal theologians will freely admit
the Bible *does* condemn modern homosexuality. Even some

gay theologians have made concessions. For example, "The four verses cited from the New Testament . . . indicate with no possibility of qualification that homosexual practices were considered by Paul (and the writer of 1 Timothy) to be concrete sins on a par with adultery and murder."[97] Such admissions do prove that when gay theology teaches these verses do *not* condemn homosexuality, the burden of proof rests with them. Has the homosexual community established its burden of proof? No! Not for a single Scripture.

14. What does the creation account teach about the homosexual lifestyle?

The Genesis accounts (Genesis 1:27; 2:18,21-24) and Matthew 19:4-6 teach that God created mankind in a specific manner (male and female) with specific purposes relative to this (marriage, sexual unity, and procreation implied).

The most proper place to begin a scriptural evaluation of homosexuality is not with the texts that reject it, but with the texts that underlie and support these condemnatory passages.[98] This background approach is something that almost all pro-homosexual writers fail to supply.

Consideration of the creation account is vital for many reasons. To begin with, it is a *creation* account. Men and women are not the blind products of a chance evolution in which literally nothing is normative and individuals are free to choose their own morality or sexuality. Men are accountable to the God who created them; they are not the products of an impersonal Nature who has no concern whatever with how they live their lives.[99]

Below are five reasons why the creation account is crucial to any scriptural discussion of homosexuality.

First, the acceptance of homosexuality violates the divinely intended order and the essence of human creation itself.

God declared that it was not good for man to be alone. To remedy this situation, God created a woman as a divine complement and counterpart to maleness. Only man and *woman* were intended to have intimate sexual fellowship. This means homosexuality distorts and disorders God's intentions in creation and that the practice of homosexuality contradicts the pattern of heterosexuality at its most basic level. Lifestyle homosexuality both denies and defies the polarities of sex in such a way that even sinful heterosexual behavior such as fornication and adultery cannot.

Second, homosexuals cannot obey God's command to procreate.

In Genesis 1:28, God commanded Adam and Eve and their descendants to "be fruitful and multiply and fill all the earth." If Adam had decided to be a homosexual, no one else would ever have been born.

Third, homosexuality constitutes a conscious rebellion against the divinely created order.

According to Romans 1:32 and other Scriptures, homosexuals know that their behavior is sinful. The continued choice to practice such activity is therefore an intentional rebellion against God and the creation order.

Fourth, the Bible is saturated with the premises of the creation account.

Were homosexuality legitimate in any manner, the Scriptures would not assume a heterosexual bias but would include the homosexual option. If God intended man to be bisexual or homosexual, or if He had created man androgynous, the fact of His creating mankind in such a manner would be evident throughout other statements in Scripture relating to the nature of man. But the only standard we find upheld is a heterosexual one. "From the first chapter of Genesis to the book of Revelation the twofold meaning of sexual-genital expression—namely, procreation and union—is clearly manifest.... Yahweh is portrayed as the faithful bridegroom, and Israel, the faithful's bride, indicating that heterosexual love can be the basis for expressing the mystery of God's loving the human race.... The author of Ephesians, moreover, reiterates the same revealed truth about human sexuality in the context of the sublime comparison in which the husband is compared with Christ and the wife with the church. When the author wishes to express the love Christ has for his church, he turns to the heterosexual love of husband and wife [Ephesians 5:25,28]."[100]

In other words, all of Scripture is impregnated with premises concerning the properness of heterosexuality; by comparison, homosexuality is conspicuously absent except by condemnation.

Fifth, homosexuality distorts the image of God.

Genesis 1:27 clearly teaches that the image of God comprises both male and female—a complementarity which is eternal and will exist forever. To affirm homosexuality as biblical and normal is to distort the image of God and by implication, to insult the nature and being of God Himself.

In understanding the divine purpose in creation and the fact that creation reflects God's own Being, we are better able to understand the reasons for the biblical condemnations of modern homosexuality and why they are severe.

15. What does the account of Sodom and Gomorrah teach about the homosexual lifestyle (Genesis 19:4-7)?

> Before [Lot and the angels (who had appeared as men) had retired], all the men from every part of the city of Sodom—both young and old—surrounded the house. They called to Lot, "Where are the men who came to you tonight? Bring them out to us so that we can have sex with them [KJV: "that we may know them"]." Lot went outside to meet them and shut the door behind him and said, "No, my friends. Don't do this wicked thing" (NIV).

Derrick Sherwin Bailey was the first modern theologian to question the traditional Jewish and Christian understanding concerning Sodom and Gomorrah. He argues the King James translation "to know" is not a reference to sexual intercourse and therefore would argue that the New International translation cited above is a poor translation. He observes that the primary meaning of the Hebrew word *yada,* "to know," means to "get acquainted with" or "having knowledge of" and has few sexual connotations. He argues that the word occurs 943 times in the Old Testament and yet is only used a dozen times to refer to sexual intercourse. "Thus it is exceptional to find *yada* employed in a coital sense."[101] Further, in those rare cases where it is so employed, it refers only to *heterosexual* intercourse.[102]

From this perspective, the Sodomites were allegedly angry with Lot for allowing strangers whose good or evil motives were unknown to enter his house. (These were the angels [Genesis 19:1] who appeared in the form of men.) Thus, the townspeople were demanding to "know" only the strangers' intent and character. (But surely if the people of

Sodom were as evil as Scripture teaches, it is doubtful their general wickedness would produce such a *moral* concern.)

First, word meaning is determined not only by definition and priority but also by general context. It is true that only about a dozen usages of *yada* in the Bible refer to sexual intercourse. However, in its immediate context (Genesis 19:5) *yada* can mean nothing other than sexual intercourse. Lot was facing an emergency. He was confused and fearful. He did not know who these angels were, but he was undoubtedly impressed with them. So he rashly offers his daughters to mollify the sexual appetites of the crowd (Genesis 19:8). Acting out of sheer desperation and hopelessness, he proposes a lesser evil (heterosexual rape) in place of a greater evil (homosexual rape).

Otherwise, why would a father offer his daughters to be raped if the Sodomites were merely violating social custom by making an impolite request to evaluate the strangers' character? The fact that Lot refers to his daughters' virgin status indicates he understood the *sexual* content of the request and therefore offered a sexual bribe. Notice also that the men were not interested in the women; they refused Lot's offer and angrily demanded their lusts be satisfied by what they thought were men (Genesis 19:9). Also, "in verse 8 the same verb [*yada*] with the negative particle is used to describe Lot's daughters as having 'not known' a man. The verb here obviously means 'have intercourse with'."[103] Clearly then, *yada* refers to sexual intercourse.

Second, additional Scriptures clearly identify the primary sin of Sodom as sexual, and significantly, as perverted sexuality. Second Peter 2:7-10 refers to the behavior of the men of Sodom as the "sensual conduct of unprincipled men" (NASB) and to their "lawless deeds," noting that God's judgment is specially reserved for "those who indulge the flesh in its corrupt desires" (NASB). Jude 7 teaches that "Sodom and Gomorrah and the cities around them ... indulged in gross immorality and went after strange flesh" (NASB).

> The term "strange flesh" could imply unnatural acts between men or even of human beings with animals. The inhabitants of Canaan were guilty of both of these sins (Leviticus 18:23-29). This definitely includes the cities of Sodom and Gomorrah. History and archaeology confirm the same conditions.[104]

Third, Jewish and Christian tradition uniformly testifies that the sin of Sodom was homosexual. For example, one rabbinic commentary notes the Sodomites had an agreement among themselves to sodomize and rob all strangers.[105] Philo, a Jew of Alexandria (25 B.C. to A.D. 45), noted that in Sodom "the men became accustomed to being treated like women."[106]

After citing numerous early sources in confirmation of this fact (Josephus, Justin Martyr, Methodius of Olympius, etc.), systematic theologian Dr. John Jefferson Davis concludes, "It is clear that both the immediate context of Genesis 19:5 and a long history of both Jewish and Christian interpretation point unmistakably to the true meaning of the text: homosexual practices. Bailey's misinterpretation of the text, which has become a stock argument in pro-homosexual circles, simply cannot be sustained."[107]

Finally, modern biblical commentators are in almost universal agreement that the sin of Sodom was homosexuality. To name but a few, Keil and Delitzsch; H.C. Leupold; J.P. Lange, and many others.[108]

In Jude 7 it is specifically stated that the destruction of Sodom and Gomorrah was both a lesson and a divine warning to all men regarding homosexuality. Who will argue that this is not the historical legacy of Sodom and Gomorrah? These are known worldwide as cities on which God visited divine judgment because of their homosexual practices. Even Bailey confesses, "This story has exercised a powerful influence, directly or indirectly, upon the civil and ecclesiastical attitudes to [homosexuality]...."[109] Indeed, if this passage never had reference to homosexuality, how did the term "sodomy" (from Sodom) become a universal synonym for homosexuality?

16. What do the Levitical passages teach about the homosexual lifestyle? (Leviticus 18:22; 20:13)

Do not lie with a man as one lies with a woman; that is detestable.... If a man lies with a man as one lies with a woman, both of them have done what is detestable. They must be put to death; their blood will be on their own heads (Leviticus 18:22; 20:13).

Critics claim that these passages do not condemn homosexuality itself on a moral basis but rather male cultic prostitution or "ritual impurity" associated with Canaanite idolatry. The argument is that because the idolatrous Canaanite religious practices that Leviticus condemns ceased thousands of years ago, they cannot logically apply to "loving, committed homosexual relationships" today. Thus homosexuals argue these verses "are historically interesting but have no contemporary relevance because of their setting in the rules for cultic purification, and because of the lack of clarity in their underlying meaning."[110]

The problem with such a view is that there is absolutely nothing in the text to substantiate it. First, even Bailey and Bishop John Shelby Spong, both ardent supporters of homosexuality, can see this. Bailey confesses, "It is hardly open to doubt that both the laws in Leviticus relate to *ordinary homosexual acts* between men, and not to ritual or other acts performed in the name of religion."[111] Spong also admits that normal homosexual practices are condemned.[112]

Second, when God wants to specifically mention the practices of cultic prostitutes, He does so, as in Deuteronomy 23:17: "No Israelite man or woman is to become a shrine prostitute." The fact they are not mentioned in Leviticus 18:22; 20:13 indicates that God is dealing with homosexuality *per se,* not with any alleged specific form of Canaanite cultic practice.

Third, the entire context of both Leviticus 18 and Leviticus 20 is primarily one of *morality,* not idolatrous worship. Thus, in Leviticus 18:1-5 God informs the Israelites they must not imitate the evil practices of the Canaanites but be careful to obey God's laws and follow His injunctions. God is driving out the Canaanites not for their idolatry but for their abominable *sexual* practices. Indeed, the entire remainder of the chapter describes almost all of these evil practices as *sexual* sins: forbidden sexual relationships among family members, sexual relations during a woman's menstrual cycle, adultery, homosexuality, and bestiality. The remainder of the chapter consists of stringent warnings *not* to be defiled by such practices. This is why God commands in verse 24: "Do not defile yourself in any of these ways."

Further, the constant repetition of the themes of defilement and abomination are repeated no less than nine times in the subsequent verses (Leviticus 18:24-29).

These Levitical passages deal with *moral* concerns, not merely the fact of participation in idolatrous Canaanite rituals. Further, such moral concerns are still relevant for today. This is why Bahnsen argues, "The predominant character of [these sections] is moral, and their content is generally recognized as binding today (e.g., prohibiting incest, adultery, child sacrifice, idolatry, oppression of the poor, slander, hatred, unjust weights and measures). . . . The defender of homosexuality must produce a viable criterion for distinguishing between moral and ceremonial laws, or else consistently reject them all."[113]

Finally, consider the lexical meaning of the Hebrew word translated "abomination" (*toebah*): "[This word is] used five times in Leviticus 18 [and] is a term of strong disapproval, meaning literally something detestable and hated by God."[114]

In conclusion, no one can logically maintain that God is not condemning homosexuality *per se* in these passages.

17. What does Romans 1 teach about the homosexual lifestyle?

Romans 1:26,27 is the major New Testament text on homosexuality; it also condemns lesbianism. Although its meaning is clear on the surface, homosexuals still argue that Paul was not condemning homosexuality *per se* but merely the Greek practice of pederasty (sodomy with a boy) or the "unnatural" practice of heterosexuals turning to homosexuality. Thus, when Paul argued homosexuality was "against nature," he was arguing only that it was against the "nature" of heterosexuals. Homosexuals, far from acting "against nature," are actually acting in harmony "with nature"—i.e., with their true homosexual/biological nature. The practice becomes *sinful* only when heterosexuals engage in homosexual activities, because for them it is unnatural. (This is like arguing that rape is moral and natural for rapists, but immoral for nonrapists.) Supposedly, because homosexuals are "born that way" homosexual practice is normal for them. But for those born heterosexual, it is a sin to practice homosexual acts. (If this is so, then what can homosexuals say about all their proselytizing activities directed at *heterosexual* boys and men?)

In addition, they contend that Paul and the other biblical writers were ignorant of the more "enlightened" scientific/theological view of homosexuality that distinguishes between the homosexual act and the homosexual condition, the latter being something for which homosexuals *have no responsibility*. But if they aren't responsible for what they *are*, how can they be responsible for what their basic nature leads them to *do*?

If such arguments have any validity whatever, one wonders why a man so erudite and discerning as the apostle Paul never made the fine distinctions cited by homosexuals. Not once does he mention pederasty, nor does he imply that he is referring only to heterosexuals who practice homosexuality. Neither does he distinguish the supposed homosexual act/condition. Paul is plainly condemning homosexuality *of itself.* The dictionary definitions of the words Paul uses— *pathe aschemosune,* etc.—clearly refer to sexual activity.[115]

The kinds of homosexual sins listed in Romans are themselves said to be the consequences of an earlier apostasy as well as divine judgment. Paul teaches a logical trend downward: 1) Men refuse to accept the intuitive knowledge which God has placed within them concerning Himself (vv. 18-22), 2) this results in rebellion against God manifested in idolatry (putting something else in God's place in our lives, whether self or various idols, v. 23), 3) God begins a process of initial judgment or "giving over" to sin (vv. 24, 25), 4) this produces, in part, unnatural lusts and perversions (vv. 26,27), and 5) results in a wide variety of additional vices and evils (vv. 28-32)—as homosexual literature and lifestyle demonstrate. As Bahnsen observes, "In response, God gives them over to impure lusts and the dishonoring of their bodies— specifically, to homosexuality, which in turn stimulates further depravities."[116] According to Colossians 3:5, greed of any type, including sexual greed, is a form of idolatry. As Dr. Davis comments in an important observation:

> It is also significant that in the Pauline analysis homosexual practices derive ultimately not from the social environment, but from the human heart or inner disposition, which is turned away from God, its ultimate good, and turned toward the mutable goods of creation, including the self. The inward and invisible apostasy of the heart eventually becomes visible in false religions and immoral, anti-social behavior. "Idolatry," notes Ernst Kasemann, "opens the floodgates for vices which destroy society and turn creation back into terrible chaos."[117]

The specific descriptions by the apostle Paul are also noteworthy. The book of Romans speaks of homosexuals burning in their lusts toward one another. The NASB states, "burned in their desire": the NIV reads, "were inflamed with lust," and the Amplified translates, "were set ablaze (burned out, consumed) with lust."

Even if these verses referred only to pederasty, they would still condemn many homosexuals today because their lust can be so consuming it often leads to child molestation even when that is not the original intent. Consider the following dialogue of the late Roger Montgomery, a former homosexual turned heterosexual, and Dr. John Ankerberg on "The John Ankerberg Show" in late 1989. As Roger explained, many, perhaps a majority, of homosexuals today were molested by an older homosexual as a child or teenager:

> *Montgomery:* I recruited younger people, but it didn't matter to me. All that mattered to me was my sexual thrill. And it didn't matter to me how it would affect anyone else's life. And knowing other homosexuals I believe the same thing is true for them. They don't care how it affects that young person's life at all.... It's like an addiction. That's why most homosexuals disagree or they would violently say, "We're not recruiters" because they don't intend to. But that doesn't negate their responsibility at all because they didn't intend to. They are still molesting our children.
>
> *Ankerberg:* What does that say then in our society about the homosexuals trying to pass laws to teach children in the schools or camps or at Sunday schools without any infringement?
>
> *Montgomery:* They are recruiters. And they're after your children and my children. And if they are allowed to continue they will achieve their goal.[118]

In other words, sexual addictions of any type can not only be extremely powerful but extremely corrupting. Because many homosexuals are literally controlled by insatiable lusts, this leads them into routine child molestation even when they never initially intended it.

But as we noted, the book of Romans also teaches that homosexuality can be a consequence of idolatry—forsaking the true God for another (false) god (Colossians 3:5). The idolatry from which the sin of homosexuality and other sins can originate is seen in homosexual literature, especially of militant lesbian feminism and gay theology. For example, consider the following statement by Sally Gearhart in her article "The Miracle of Lesbianism."

> We have been teased, cajoled, flattered, humiliated and even threatened—not to say actually physically coerced—into believing in the eternal, external and exclusive existence of the great father-god, and in the man-made theological fabrications that surround his

name. In serving the external god, we have neglected...
the woman-god, however she is named, who speaks not
from outside but from within us....[119]

Gearhart also refers to the Christian concept of God as
something evil and calls for a return to the feminine god-
dess of witchcraft: Having suppressed the truth in unrigh-
teousness, having abandoned the innate knowledge that
God has placed within them, the homosexual or lesbian has
been "given over" to his or her sin: This is the process
described in Romans.

But worse, the apostle further teaches that homosexuals
are "without excuse" because they intuitively realize such
acts are wrong and *are* worthy of death (Romans 1:32). Yet
they deliberately suppress such knowledge (Romans 1:18).
They not only suppress this knowledge, but in spite of all
they continue their practices and even encourage others to
do so, giving their hearty approval (Romans 1:28-32).

Homosexuality involves a willful violation of the fundamental moral law of God, which is known instinctively by
all men in all cultures because God Himself has placed such
knowledge in the hearts of all men and women. God Himself has been their teacher as to the knowledge of Him, and
so there is no possibility of failure here. This is undoubtedly
the reason why every culture has condemned homosexuality and why such knowledge must be suppressed in
order to be justified.

18. What does 1 Corinthians 6:9-11 teach about the homosexual lifestyle?

1 Corinthians 6:9-10

> Do not be deceived: Neither the sexually immoral nor
> idolaters nor adulterers nor male prostitutes nor
> homosexual offenders nor thieves nor the greedy nor
> drunkards nor slanderers nor swindlers will inherit
> the kingdom of God.

Homosexuals have maintained that this passage is
either mistranslated or culturally restricted. Some have
claimed that the word *malakos* (translated "male prostitutes") refers only to a general moral weakness with no
specific reference to homosexuality and that *arsenokoitai*
(translated "homosexual offenders") refers to male prostitutes—and thus once again these verses are not condemning modern "loving" homosexual unions.[120]

But *malakoi* and *arsenokoitai* have specific meanings. The former literally means "soft to the touch."[121] In Greek culture it was used metaphorically for males who partook of the passive role in the homosexual act. The second term, *arsenokoitai,* also clearly refers to homosexual relationships—specifically, to the person who took the active role in the homosexual act.

In *arsenokoitai, arsen* refers to a "male" and *koitai* to "bed"—a word with clear sexual connotations (cf. Hebrews 13:4). In other words, this term refers to males who go to bed with other males. Or in the words of *Thayer's Greek-English Lexicon,* "One who lies with a male as with a female."[122]

Further, the entire section of 1 Corinthians 6:9ff is highlighted by the word *adiaoi*—"the unrighteous." The terms referring to homosexuality are found in connection with additional sexual sins—fornicators (*pornoi*) and adulterers (*moichoin*). In other words, the meanings of the words themselves and their context all argue for relevance to homosexual practices today. Unrepentant homosexuality, fornication, and adultery *all* exclude one from the kingdom of God.[123]

19. What do 2 Peter 2:1-10 and Jude teach about the homosexual lifestyle?

These passages are replete with references to homosexuality and, by implication, to the Christian homosexual movement as well. The parallels to the passage in Romans are noteworthy. In 2 Peter 2, observe that the context involves "false teachers among you" (i.e., within the church) who will secretly (slyly) introduce "destructive heresies" even denying the Master (Jesus) who bought them. Notice in addition, that many will follow their "sensuality" (NASB, v. 2) or "shameful ways," and that because of such false teachers the way of truth will be "maligned" or distorted.

Such persons are said to be full of greed and described as those who exploit Christians with "false words" (NASB, v. 3) or "stories."

So far the passage is applicable to both homosexuals and Christian homosexuals who promote the kinds of arguments we have been considering in this book. Notice also that in this passage it is *homosexuality* which is directly cited as an illustration of all the above. Sodom and Gomorrah are specifically stated to have been destroyed as "*an example* to those who would live ungodly thereafter."

The book of Jude continues to reject homosexuality:

In a similar way, Sodom and Gomorrah and the surrounding towns gave themselves up to sexual immorality and perversion. They serve as an example of those who suffer the punishment of eternal fire.... These dreamers pollute their own bodies, reject authority and...speak abusively against whatever they do not understand.... These are the very things that destroy them....

These are men who divide you, who follow mere natural instincts and do not have the Spirit (Jude 7-19).

These words are self-explanatory and require little comment.

We have now examined the major direct scriptural verses relating to homosexuality. The one who claims that the biblical case against homosexuality is based on a few "isolated" and "obscure" prooftexts simply does not understand the weight of these Scriptures. Besides the above verses, there are literally scores of additional Scriptures which are *applicable* to homosexual practices even though the term itself is not used (for example, Romans 6:11-21; 12:1,2; 1 Corinthians 6:19,20; Philippians 1:20; Colossians 3:5-8; Revelation 21:8).

In conclusion, both the Christian church and society do great harm to people—homosexuals and heterosexuals—when they actively promote the cause of homosexuality in America.

Conclusion:
How do I leave the homosexual lifestyle?

Leaving the homosexual lifestyle may be relatively easy or difficult depending upon a number of factors. The most important step is this—accepting that the homosexual lifestyle is morally wrong and resolving to change. As we have documented in this booklet, change *is* clearly possible for homosexuals who want to change, and God will grant grace and power for those who turn to Him in faith with a desire to please Him in their sexual behavior. Thus, a prayer of repentance before God, resolving to leave the homosexual lifestyle, and encouragement and counsel from those who have already done so, are key.

Exodus International is one major organization devoted to helping homosexual men and women through the transition to a lifestyle of celibacy and the transition to heterosexuality. Their address is:

44

Exodus International
P.O. Box 2121
San Rafael, CA 94912
(415) 454-1017

For those who truly desire to leave the homosexual lifestyle we recommend the following prayer:

Dear God:

I now recognize that my homosexuality has been
displeasing to You. I confess my sin before You and
ask for Your power and grace to finally and com-
pletely remove myself from my previous lifestyle. I
understand that You are holy and that my sin has
separated me from You. Therefore, I now receive
Christ as my personal Lord and Savior, believing that
He died on the cross for all my sins and that He rose
from the dead three days later. I thank You that by
faith in Your Son I can now know that all of my sins
have been forgiven—past, present, and future. I no
longer need to fear Your judgment because of what
Christ has accomplished on the cross. With Your help,
I now resolve to seek any help or counseling necessary
to obey Your will for my life. In Jesus' name, Amen.

Those who prayed this prayer should understand that
commitment to Christ is a serious matter and involves
making Him Lord of every area in your life. You should also
know that same sex inclinations may, but probably will not,
automatically cease. Homosexual sin is the same as any
other sexual sin and will require time and patience to master. Another important step is a clean and permanent break
with all ties to the homosexual community, including, if
necessary, all former friendships. No avenue of temptation
should be allowed. All denial of sin is ultimately self-denial
and, of course, painful, but the mere fact of difficulty does
not excuse us from our responsibility before God to love Him
as He loved us. Thousands of gay men and women have
testified that there is victory—complete victory—and
those who have just begun their new lifestyle should be
encouraged by this fact. Books such as *Coming Out of
Homosexuality* (InterVarsity) and *Desires in Conflict* (Harvest House) will also be helpful.

Notes

1. John Leo, "On Society: Pedophiles in the Schools," *U.S. News and World Report*, October 11, 1993, p. 37.
2. Stanley Monteith, *AIDS: The Unnecessary Epidemic* (Sevierville, TN: Covenant House, 1992).
3. E.g., *Time*, June 27, 1994, p. 57.
4. Warren J. Gadpaille, "Cross-Species and Cross-Cultural Contributions to Understanding Homosexual Activity," *Archives of General Psychiatry*, Vol. 37, 1980, p. 352.
5. John Ankerberg, John Weldon, *The Myth of Safe Sex* (Chicago, IL: Moody, 1993).
6. These figures are based on Centers for Disease Control estimates roughly extrapolated from December 1993 figures, the latest available as of June 29, 1994. The 50,000 figure is conservatively extrapolated from Stanley Monteith, M.D., *HIV Watch*, Vol. 2, no. 1, p. 7. The 2 million figure is not necessarily a CDC estimate, although many authorities consider it low.
7. Press release, "AIDS in the World" (Boston, MA: International AIDS Center, Harvard School of Public Health, 1992), June 12, 1992, p. 4.
8. Stanley K. Monteith, M.D., *HIV Watch*, Vol. 2, no. 1, p. 1 (P.O. Box 1835, Soquel, CA 95073).
9. Press coverage of the French situation was extensive in the U.S.; for the American situation, e.g., the Red Cross, cf. the *Chattanooga Free-Press*, May 15, 1994, A9.
10. *Time*, June 27, 1994, pp. 55,57.
11. William Dannemeyer, *Shadow in the Land* (San Francisco, CA: Ignatius Press, 1989), p. 15.
12. *Time*, June 27, 1994, p. 58.
13. cf., Dannemeyer, *Shadow*, p. 15; Paul Cameron, *Exposing the AIDS Scandal* (Lafayette, LA: Huntington House, 1988), p. 42.
14. U.S. Government Printing Office, *Report of the Secretaries Task Force on Youth Suicide*, DHHS Publication #(ADMN)89-1621; 4 volumes, 888 pages, released August 1989. Some key citations were given *Family Research*, Summer 1989, pp. 1-7.
15. *Time*, June 27, 1994, p. 55.
16. This quotation was widely reported in the popular press in mid-1994.
17. Ankerberg and Welson, passim.
18. Enrique Rueda, *The Homosexual Network* (Old Greenwich, CT: Devin Adair Co., 1982), pp. 140,385.
19. Patrick Dixon, *The Truth About AIDS* (Nashville, TN: Nelson, 1989), p. 22.
20. *Record*, the four-page newsletter of "Evangelicals Concerned," 1st quarter, 1987, p. 70.
21. *Record*, see all issues between 1987-1990.
22. Charles W. Socarides, "Sexual Politics and Scientific Logic: The Issue of Homosexuality," *The Journal of Psychohistory*, Winter 1992, pp. 308-329.
23. Monteith, *AIDS: The Unnecessary Epidemic*, pp. 13-56; *HIV Watch*, P.O. Box 1835, Soquel, CA 95073, Vols. I and II.
24. Dannemeyer, *Shadow*, p. 17.
25. John Jefferson Davis, *Evangelical Ethics: Issues Facing the Church Today* (Phillipsburg, NJ: Presbyterian and Reformed, 1985), p. 127; *Time*, June 27, 1994, p. 57; Cameron, *Exposing*, pp. 141-143.
26. *Time*, June 26, 1994, p. 59.
27. Cameron, *Exposing the Aids Scandal* (Lafayette, LA: Huntington House, 1988), p. 42.
28. Ibid., p. 153.
29. In Dannemeyer, *Shadow*, pp. 49-50.
30. Interview conducted Feb. 26, 1992, emphasis added.
31. "Homosexual Brains," *Family Research Report*, June/September, 1991. See the evaluation of the original report in *Science* magazine, available from the Family Research Institute, P.O. Box 2091, Washington, D.C. 20013.
32. Dr. Joseph Nicolosi, taped interview for "The John Ankerberg Show."
33. Dr. Charles Socarides, taped interview for "The John Ankerberg Show," emphasis added.
34. Dr. Kenneth Klivington, in *Newsweek*, February 24, 1992.
35. The homosexual reporter M. Botkin concedes this in "Salk and Pepper," *Bay Area Reporter*, September 5, 1991, pp. 21,24, cf., "Homosexual Brains," *Family Research Report*, June/September 1991, p. 1.
36. *Newsweek*, February 24, 1992.
37. Ibid.
38. Dr. Joseph Nicolosi, taped interview for "The John Ankerberg Show."
39. See "Twins Born Gay?" *Family Research Report*, January/February 1992, pp. 1-4 and other materials from the Family Research Institute, Washington, D.C.
40. Richard A. Cohen, in *Perpetuating Homosexual Myths* (Seattle, WA: Public Education Committee, 1992 rev.), pp. 18-19.
41. Dr. Simon LeVay, taped interview for "The John Ankerberg Show."

42. See "Twins Born Gay?" p. 4.
43. Editorial, "Genetic Linkage and Male Homosexual Orientation: Reasons to be Cautious," *British Medical Journal*, August 7, 1993, p. 337, emphasis added.
44. Thanks to Dr. Paul Cameron, "Chromosomal Differences in Gays?" prepublication copy of *Family Research Report*, 1993.
45. Ibid.
46. Ibid.
47. Editorial, *British Medical Journal*, August 7, 1993, p. 337.
48. Ibid., p. 338.
49. Cameron, "Chromosomal Difference in Gays?"
50. Ibid.
51. Ibid.
52. "Can Gays and Lesbians Go Straight?" "Geraldo," June 11, 1991, transcript #974, pp. 6, 17-18, emphasis added.
53. Ibid., p. 5.
54. Ibid., p. 10.
55. Dr. Joseph Nicolosi, taped interview for "The John Ankerberg Show."
56. Cited by W.B. Pomeroy in *Dr. Kinsey and the Institute for Sex Research* (New York: Harper & Row, 1972), p. 147.
57. Cited in van den Aardweg, *Homosexuality and Hope* (Ann Arbor, MI: Servant, 1985), p. 32.
58. William Masters, V.E. Johnson, R.C. Kolodny, *Human Sexuality* (Boston: Little, Brown and Company, 1984), pp. 319-320.
59. In Judd Marmor, ed., *Homosexual Behavior: A Modern Reappraisal* (New York: Basic Books, 1980), pp. 9,66.
60. In *USA Today*, March 1, 1989, p. 4D; from *The Gay Church* by Enroth (Grand Rapids, MI, Eerdmans, 1974).
61. William Byne and Bruce Parsons, *Archives of General Psychiatry*, March 1993, cited in *Family Research Report*, March/April 1993, p. 1.
62. Editorial, *British Medical Journal*, August 7, 1993, p. 337.
63. Ibid; cf. note 4.
64. Leland E. Hinsie and Robert Jean Campbell, *Psychiatric Dictionary*, 4th ed. (New York: Oxford University Press, 1970), p. 350, emphasis added.
65. In Clifford Wilson, *Important Facts About Sex Differences* (Dandenong, Victoria, Australia: Pacific College, Inc., 1986), p. 75.
66. Clifford Allen, *Textbook for Psychosexual Disorders* (Oxford: 1962), p. 170, cited in Ed Hurst and Dave and Neta Jackson, *Overcoming Homosexuality*, p. 91, emphasis added; cf. van den Aardweg, pp. 28-33.
67. Wainwright Churchill, *Homosexual Behavior Among Males*, 1967, p. 101, cited in Dannemeyer, *Shadow in the Land*, p. 47.
68. A.P. Bell, M.S. Weinberg, and S.K. Hammersmith, *Sexual Preference Statistical Appendix* (Bloomington, IN: Indiana University Press, 1981), p. 113.
69. Paul Cameron et al, "Sexual Orientation and Sexually Transmitted Disease," *The Nebraska Medical Journal*, August 1985, rpt.
70. van den Aardweg, *Homosexuality and Hope*, p. 45.
71. Joe Dallas, "Born Gay?," *Christianity Today*, June 22, 1992, p. 23.
72. See "Born That Way?" *Family Research Report Special Report*, 1991, and updates.
73. A.P. Bell, M.S. Weinberg, and S.K. Hammersmith, *Sexual Preference*, p. 261.
74. Douglas A. Houck, "Case Study Analysis of Homosexual to Heterosexual Transformation with Overview of the Moberly Model" (Seattle, WA: Metanoya Ministries, 1988) in Cohen, *Perpetuating Homosexual Myths*, p. 9.
75. Cohen, in *Perpetuating Homosexual Myths*, p. 9.
76. Dr. Joseph Nicolosi, taped interview for "The John Ankerberg Show."
77. *The Phil Donahue Show*, Nov. 1, 1993.
78. Family Research Institute, *What Causes Homosexuality?*, p. 5.
79. Cited in *USA Today*, April 15, 1993.
80. Family Research Institute, *What Causes Homosexuality and Can It Be Cured?* (Washington, DC: Family Research Institute), p. 5.
81. In Joe Dallas, *Desires in Conflict*, p. 116, citing Irving Bieber "Male Homosexuality" *Canadian Journal of Psychiatry*, Vol. 24, no. 5, 1979, p. 416.
82. Dr. Charles Socarides, taped interview for "The John Ankerberg Show."
83. Cf. "Homosexuality: The 10% Lie," *Family Research Report*, May-June 1992 and recent materials from the Family Research Institute.
84. As reported in *The Wall Street Journal*, March 31, 1993. See also Judith A. Reisman, Edward W. Eichel, et. al., Kinsey, *Sex and Fraud: The Indoctrination of a People* (Lafayette, LA: Huntington House, 1990).
85. E.g. Michael R. Saia, *Counseling the Homosexual* (Minneapolis, MN: Bethany, 1988), pp. 41-2.
86. Roger Montgomery, *My Life in Homosexuality*, ms., 1989, pp. 43-44.
87. Jones, p. 29.
88. John Weldon, *Homosexuality: A Scientific, Biblical and Social Critique*, ms., 1992; research from Family Research Institute, P. O. Box 2091, Washington, D.C. 20013; e.g., cf. Saia, passim.

89. Saia, *Counseling*, p. 39.
90. Rueda, *Homosexual Network*, p. 296-297.
91. Program 6 of the Bishop John Spong/Walter Martin, November 1989 debate conducted on "The John Ankerberg Show."
92. See research from the Family Research Institute, Washington, D.C.
93. Weldon, *Homosexuality*, ms.
94. See Notes 42,93.
95. Ibid.
96. Cf. J. D. Unwin, "Monogamy as a Condition of Social Energy," *Hibbet Journal*, Vol. 25 (1927), pp. 662-677.
97. S. Gearhart and W. R. Johnson (eds.), *Loving Women/Loving Men: Gay Liberation in the Church* (San Francisco: Glide Publications, 1974), p. 40.
98. John Stott, "Homosexual Partnerships," Involvement, Vol. 2, p. 226.
99. See John Ankerberg, John Weldon, *The Facts On Creation vs. Evolution* (Eugene, OR: Harvest House, 1993).
100. John F. Harvey, *The Homosexual Person* (San Francisco: Ignatius, 1987), p. 95-97.
101. D. Sherwin Bailey, *Homosexuality and the Western Christian Tradition* (Hamden, CT: Shoe String Press/Archon Books, 1975 [orig. pub. London: Longman Greens & Co., 1955]), p. 3.
102. Ibid., p. 5.
103. Kidner, cited in P. Michael Uklaja, "Homosexuality and the Old Testament," *Bibliotheca Sacra*, July-Sept. 1983, p. 261.
104. Ibid., p. 262.
105. Davis, *Evangelical Ethics*, p. 116.
106. Ibid.
107. Ibid., p. 117.
108. See the commentaries on Genesis by these authors as well as G. Alders, James M. Boyce, and F.F. Bruce.
109. Bailey, *Homosexuality and the Western Christian Tradition*, p. 1.
110. Gearhart and Johnson, *Loving Women/Loving Men*, p. 40.
111. Bailey, *Homosexuality and the Western Christian Tradition*, p. 30, emphasis added.
112. "Martin/Spong Debate on Sexual Ethics," transcript from "The John Ankerberg Show," 1989.
113. Bahnsen, p. 39-40.
114. In Davis, *Evangelical Ethics*, p. 117.
115. See eg., *Thayer's Greek-English Lexicon of the New Testament*.
116. Greg L. Bahnsen, *Homosexuality: A Biblical View* (Nutley, NJ: Presbyterian and Reformed, 1981), p. 48.
117. Davis, *Evangelical Ethics* p. 120.
118. "AIDS, Homosexuality and the Power of Christ," transcript of interview conducted for "The John Ankerberg Show," 1989.
119. Gearhart and Johnson, *Loving Women/Loving Men* p. 150.
120. John Boswell, *Christianity, Social Intolerance and Homosexuality* (Chicago: University of Chicago Press, 1980), pp. 340-353.
121. *Thayer's Greek-English Lexicon*, p. 387.
122. Ibid., p. 75.
123. Bahnsen, pp. 89-91.

Other books by
John Ankerberg and John Weldon